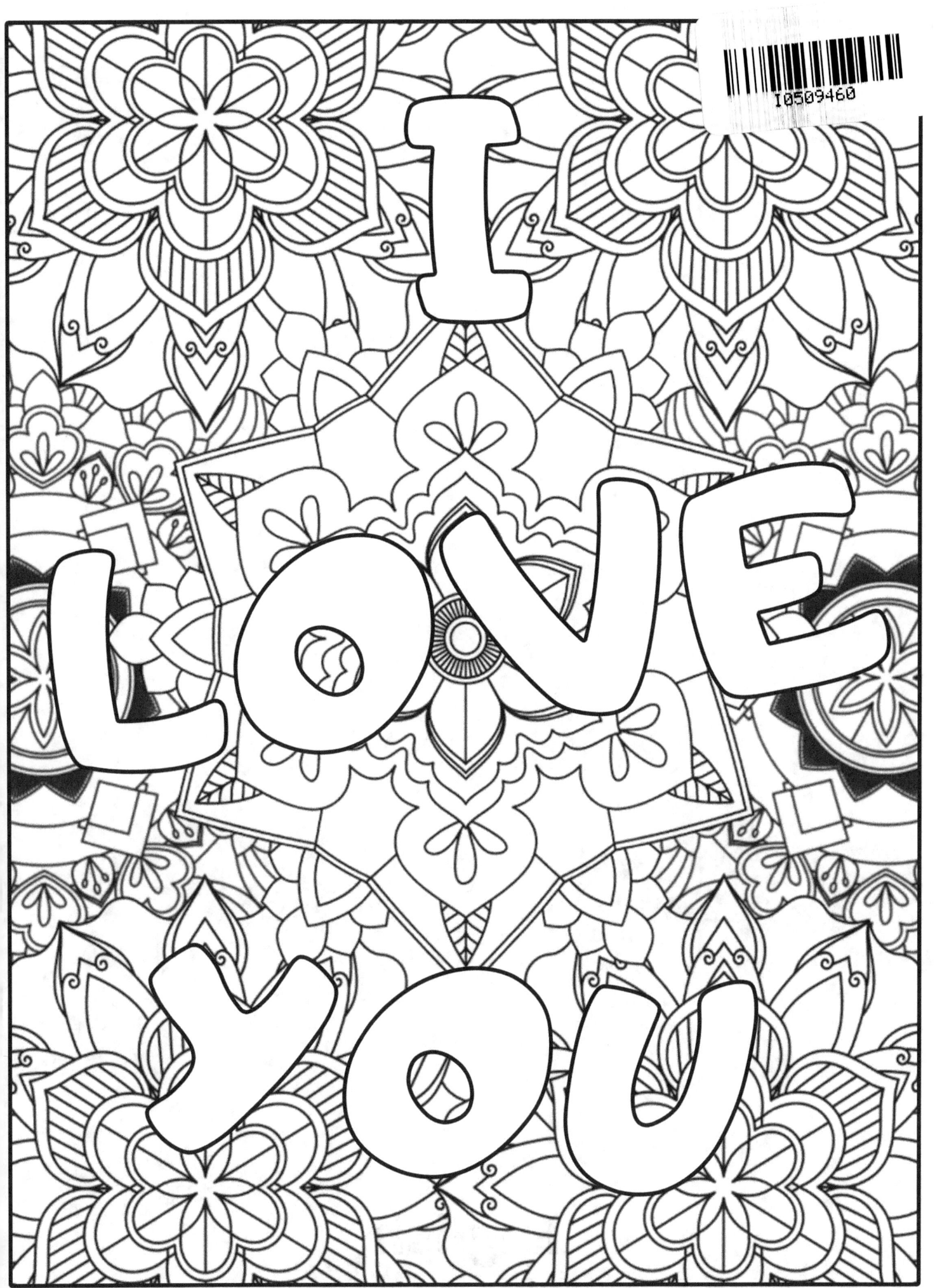

English

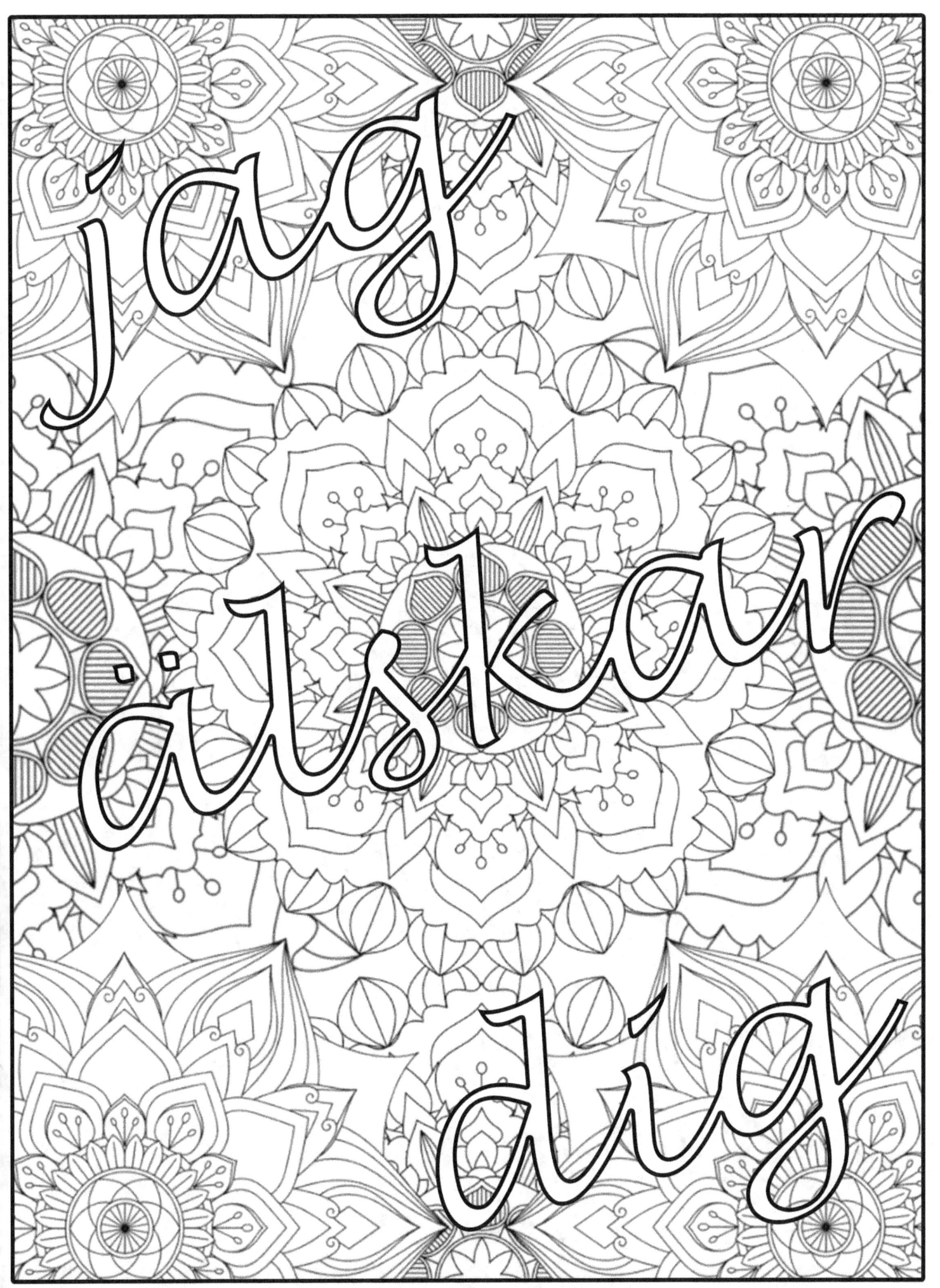

Swedish

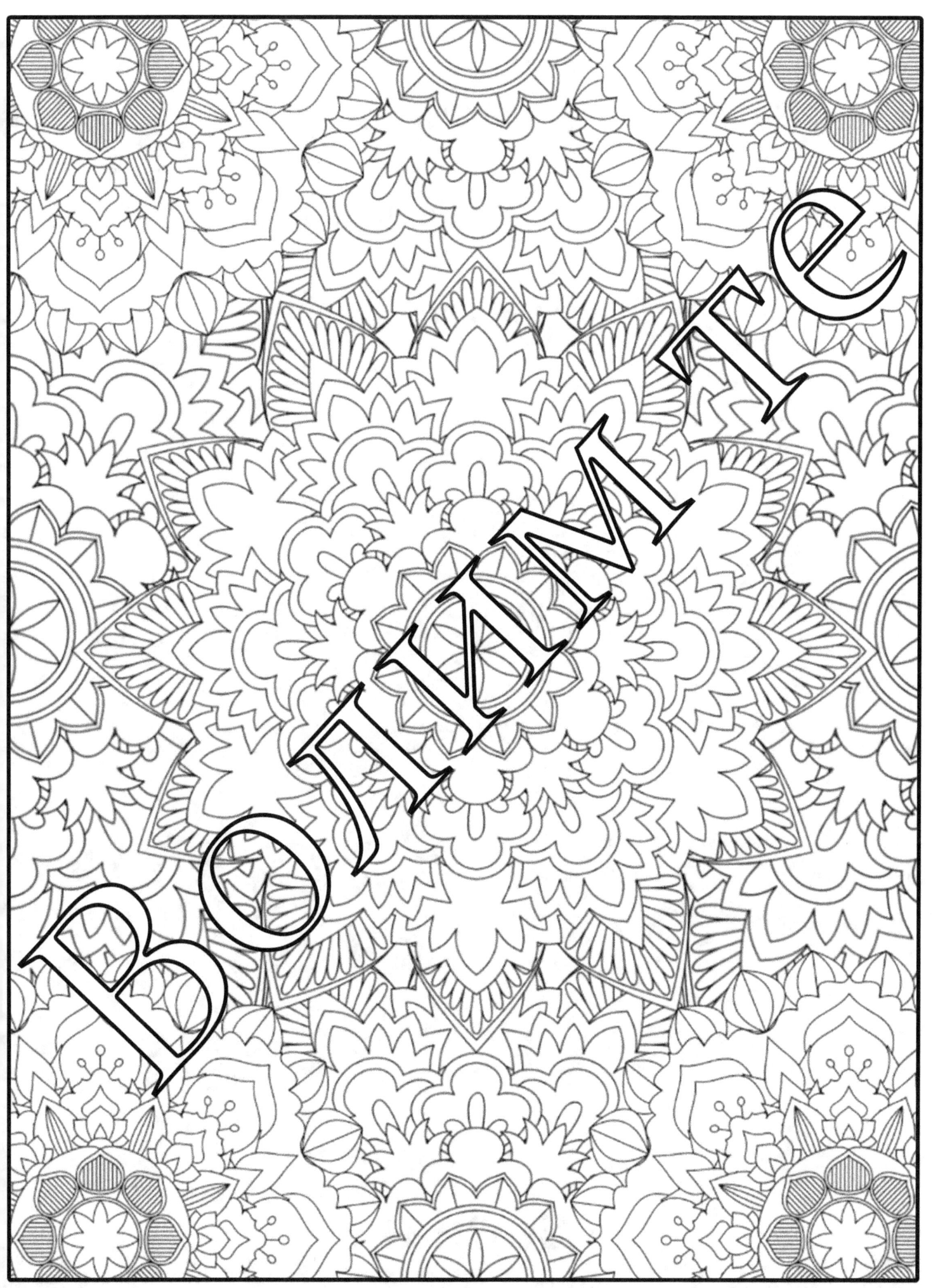

Serbian

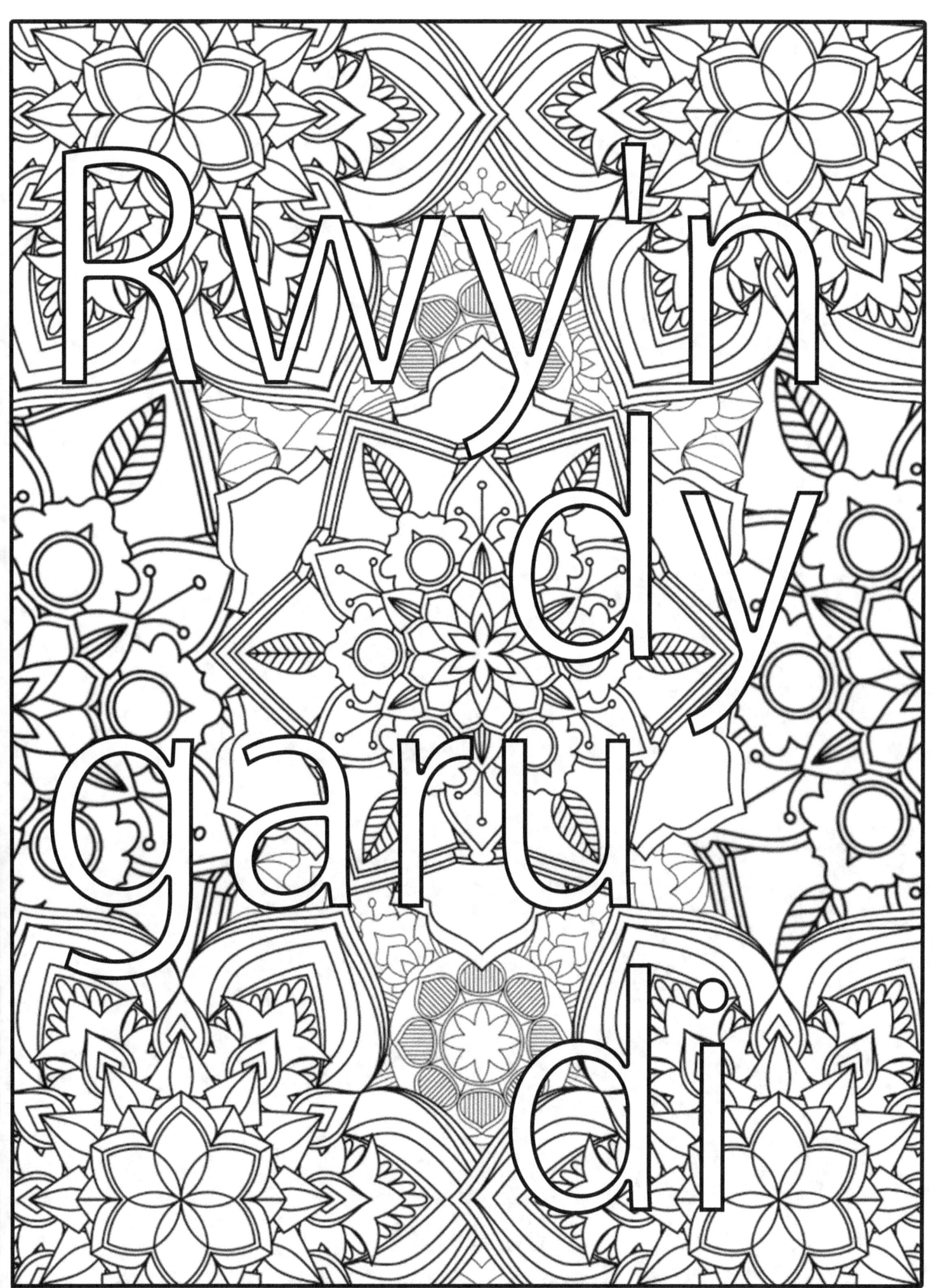

Welsh

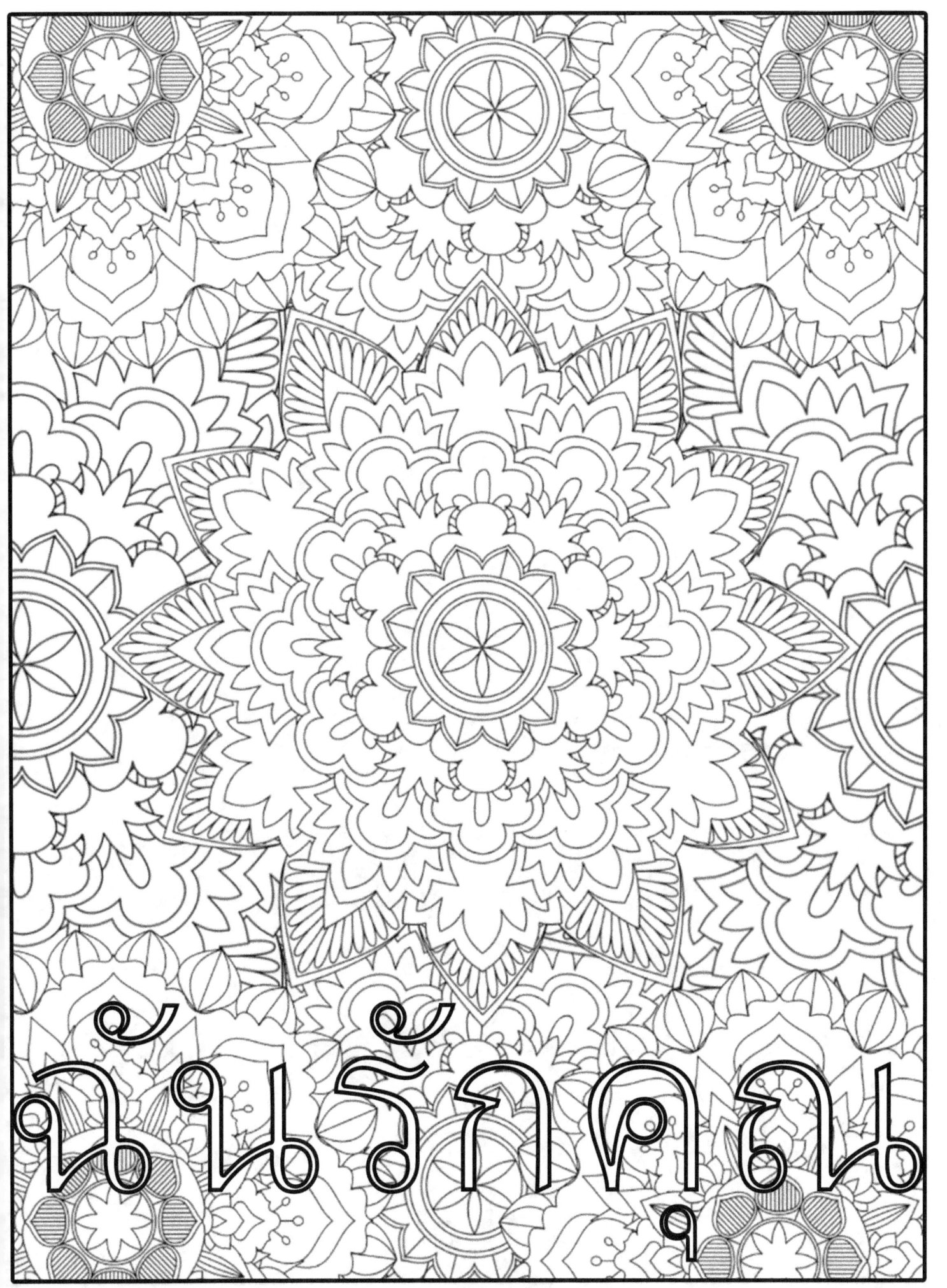

Thai

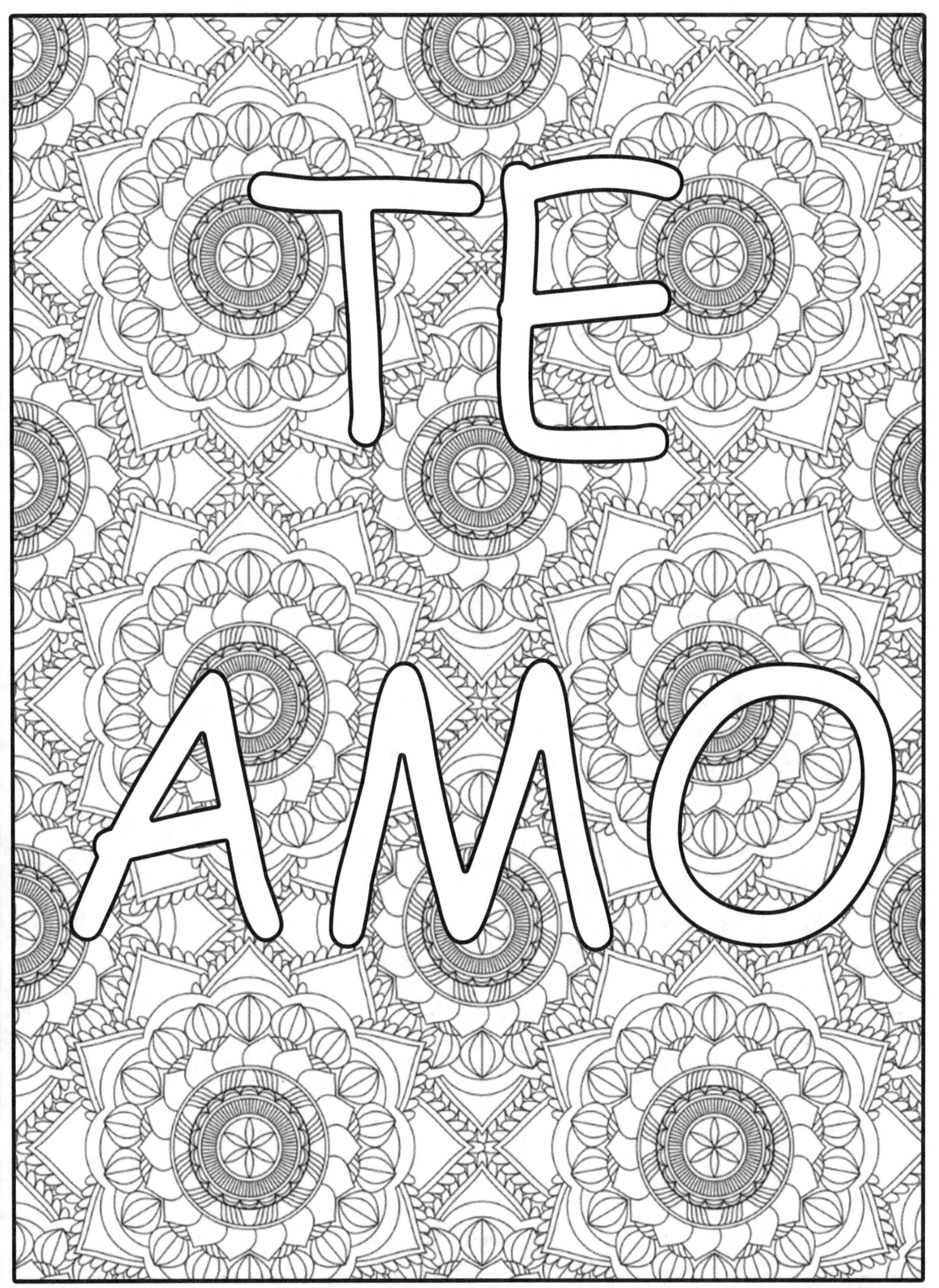

Spanish

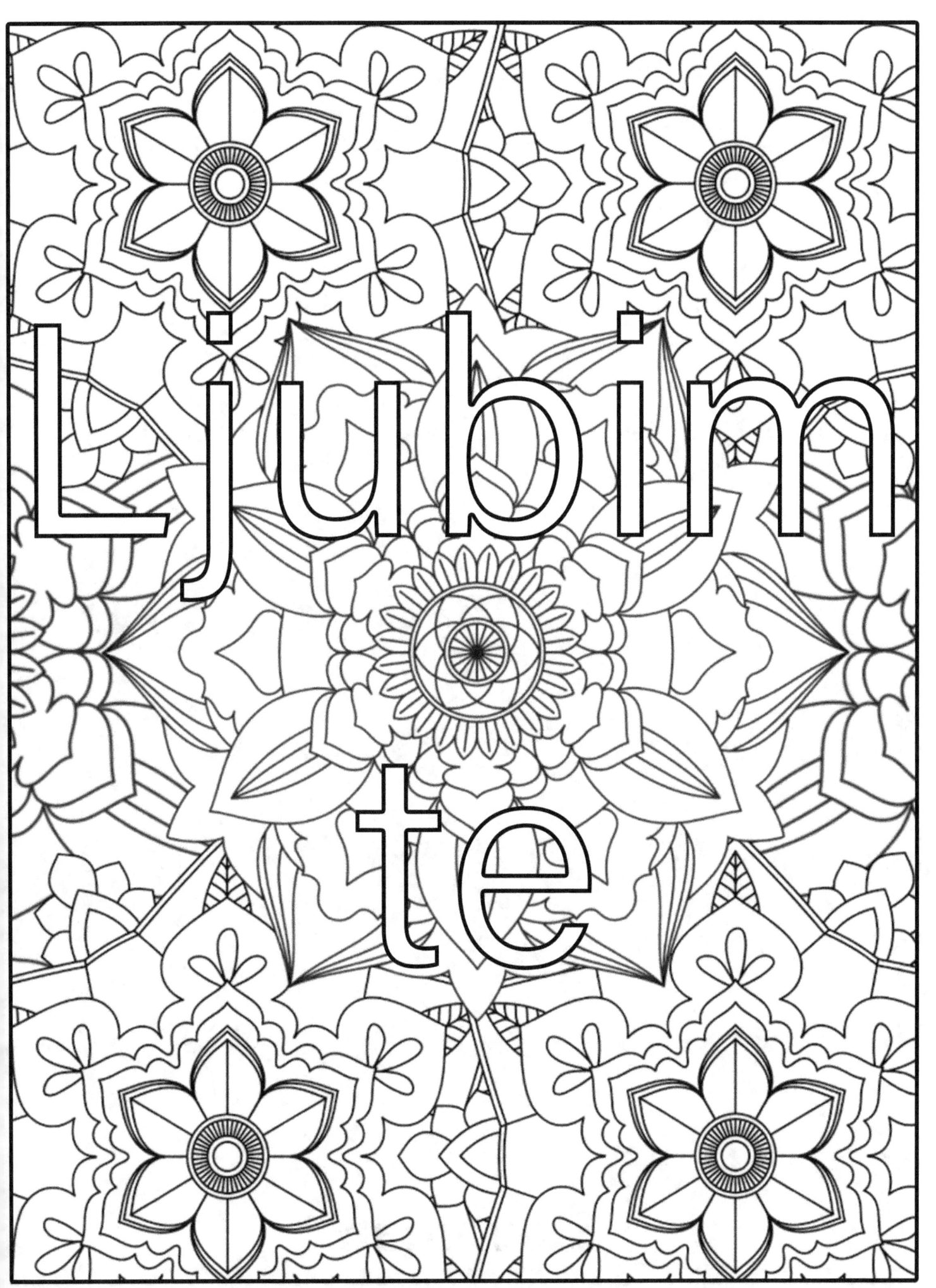

Slovenian

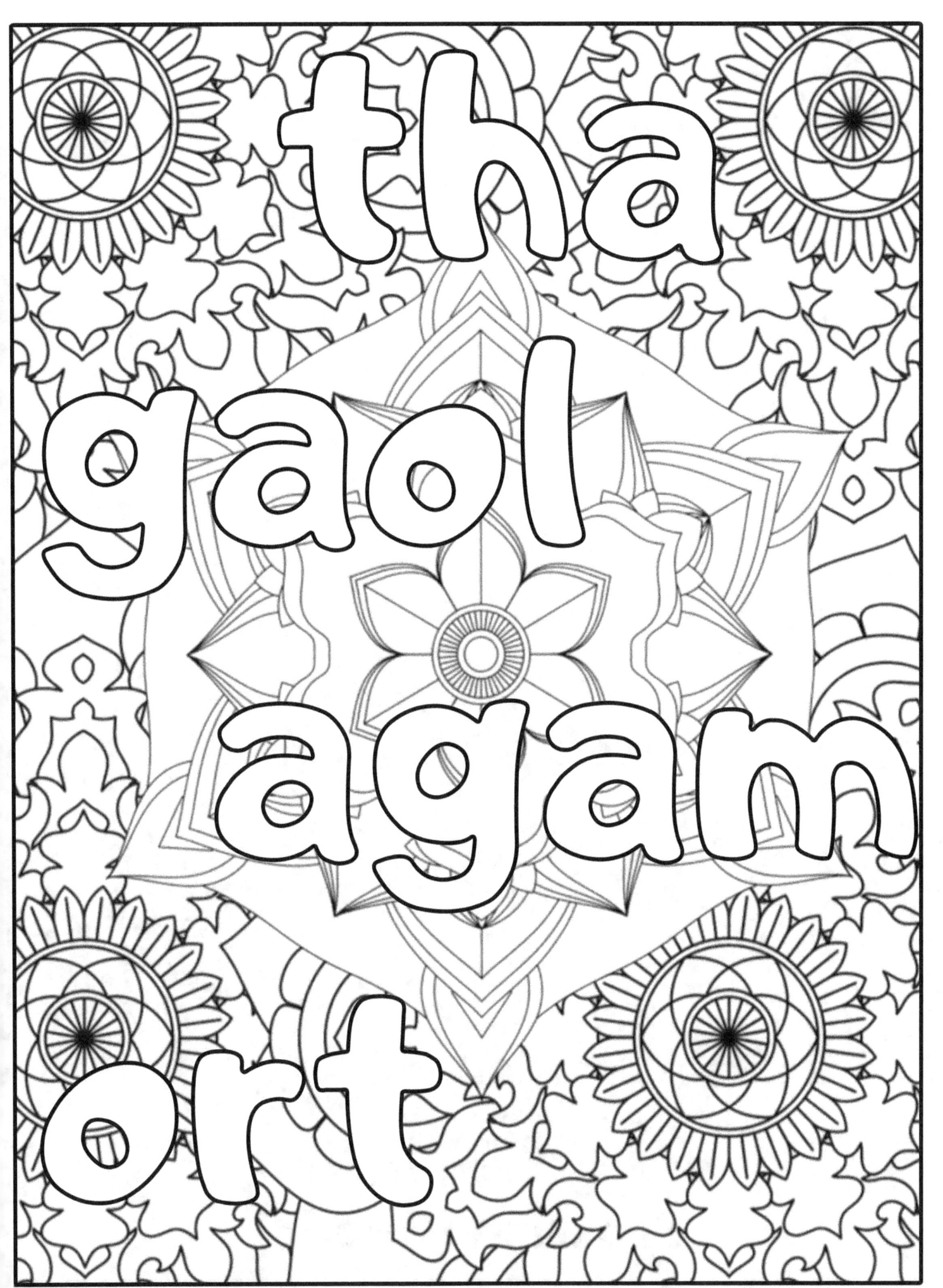

Scottish (Gaelic)

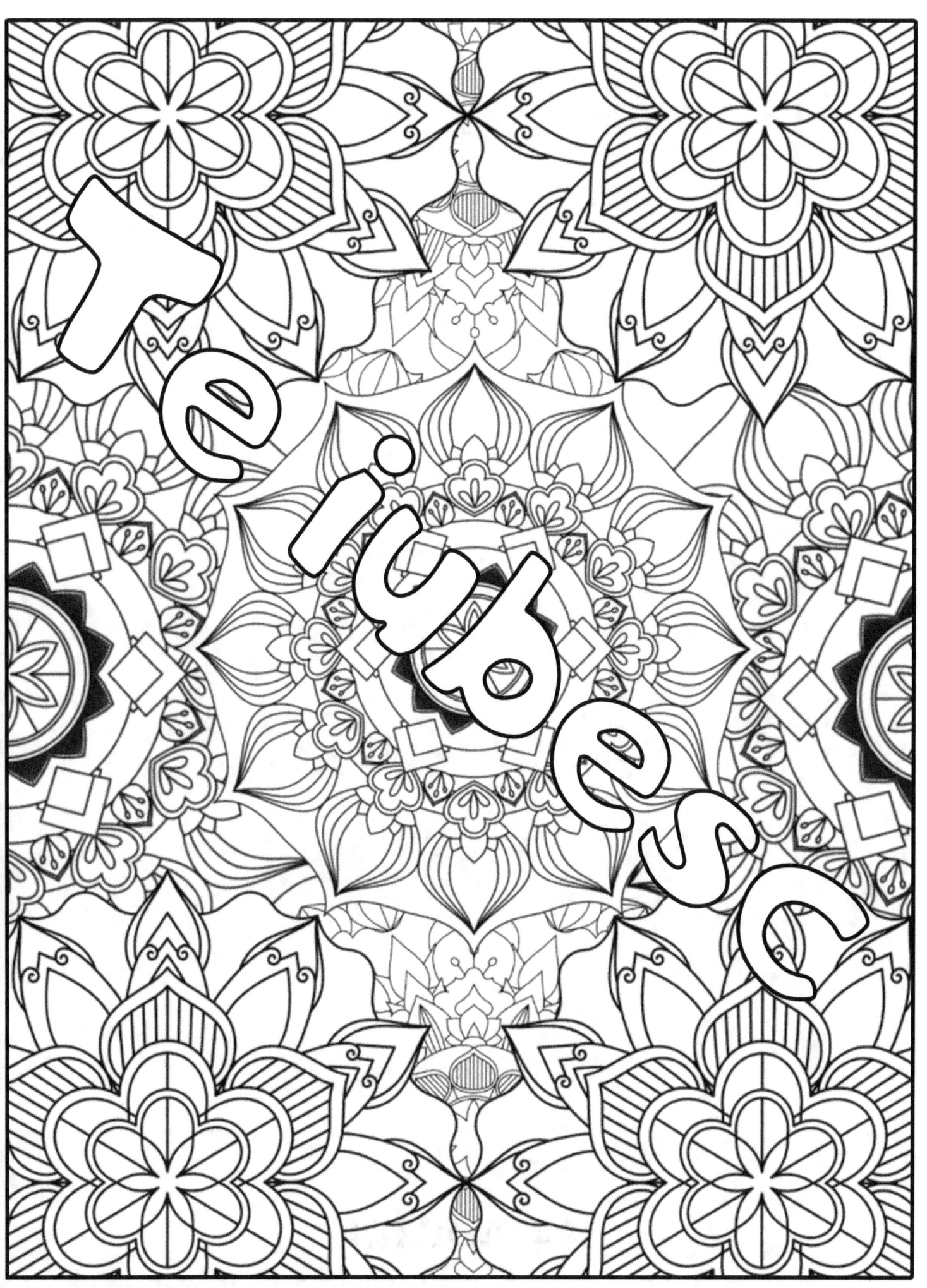

Romanian

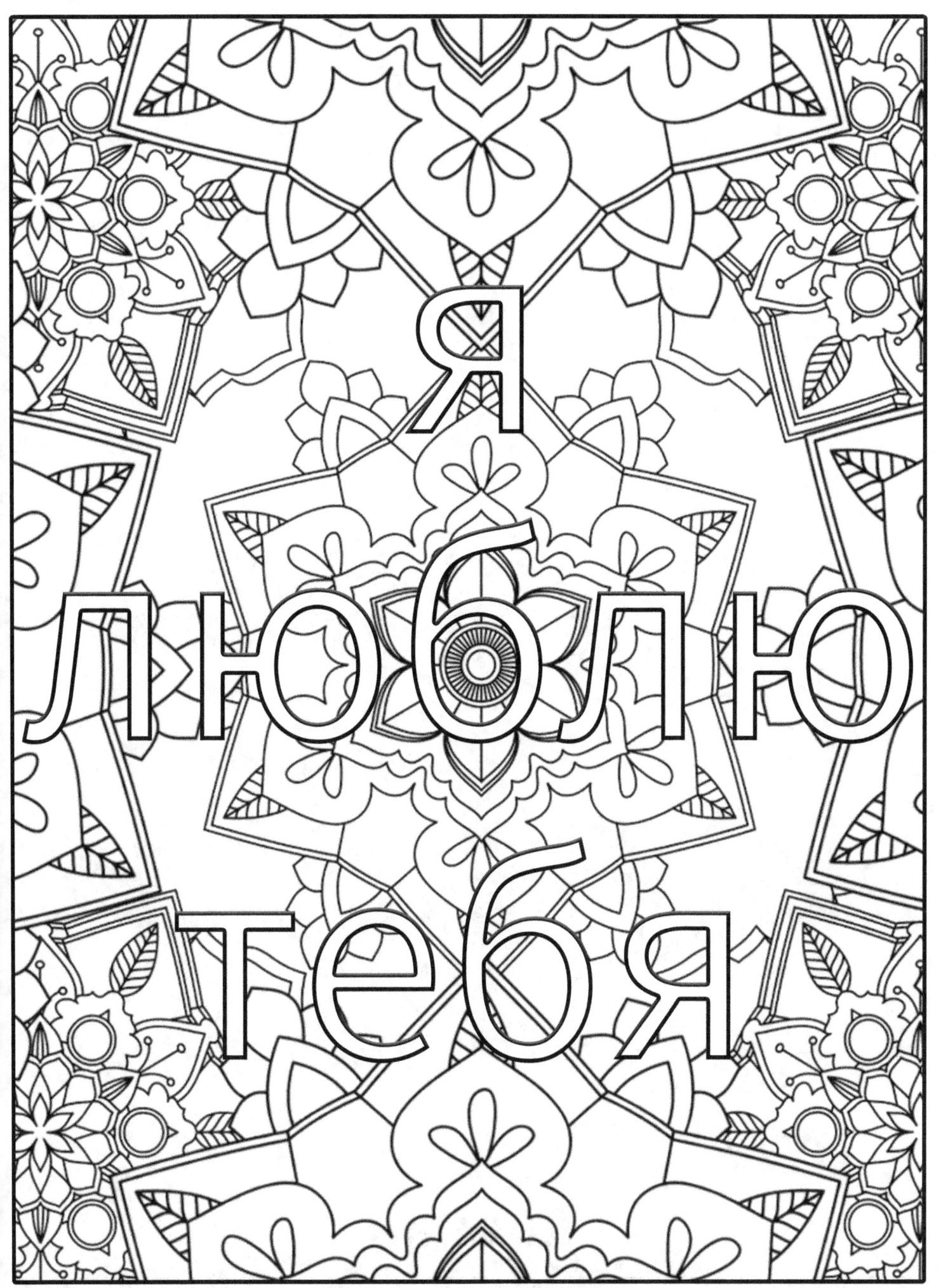

Russian

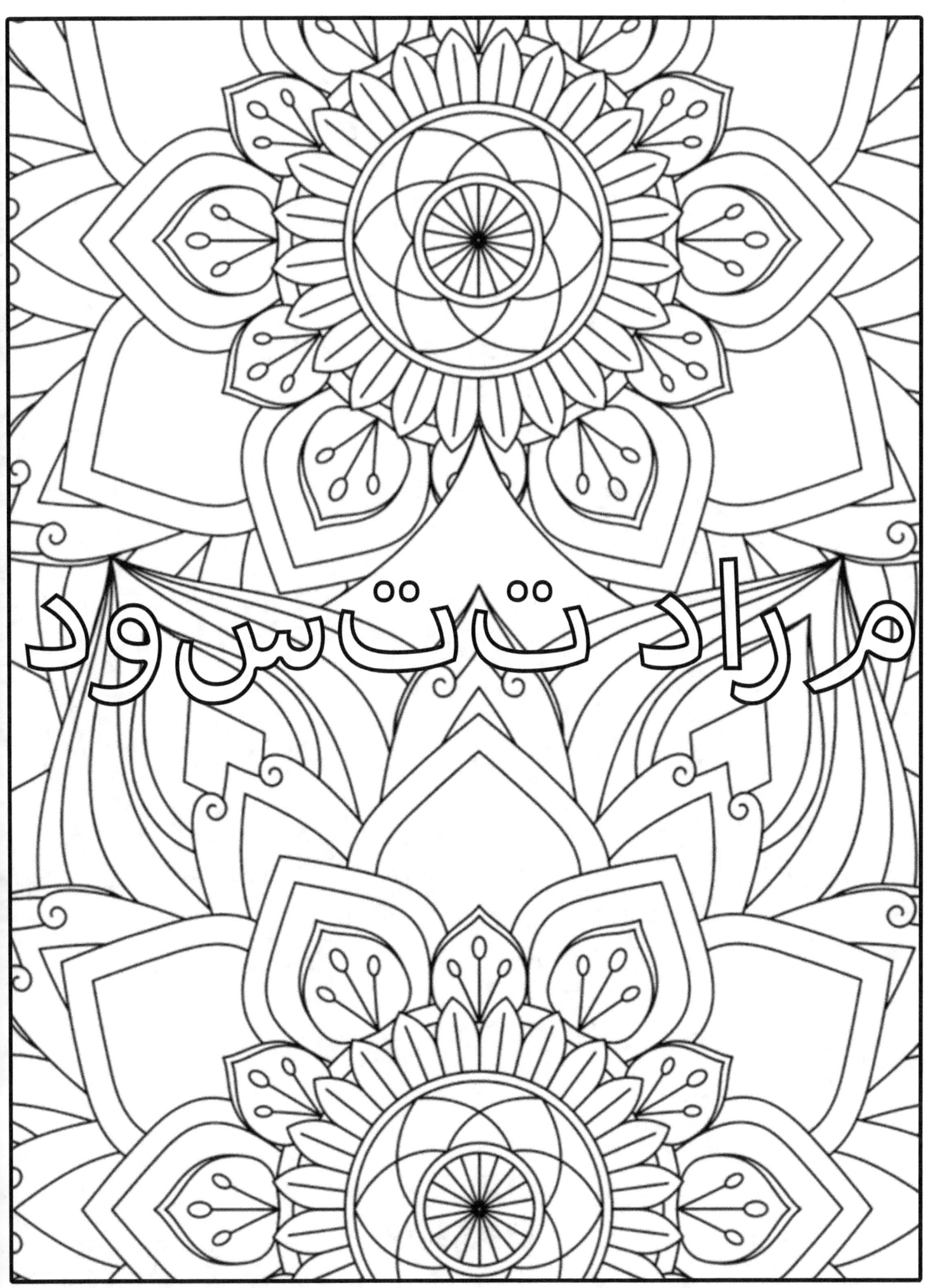

Persian

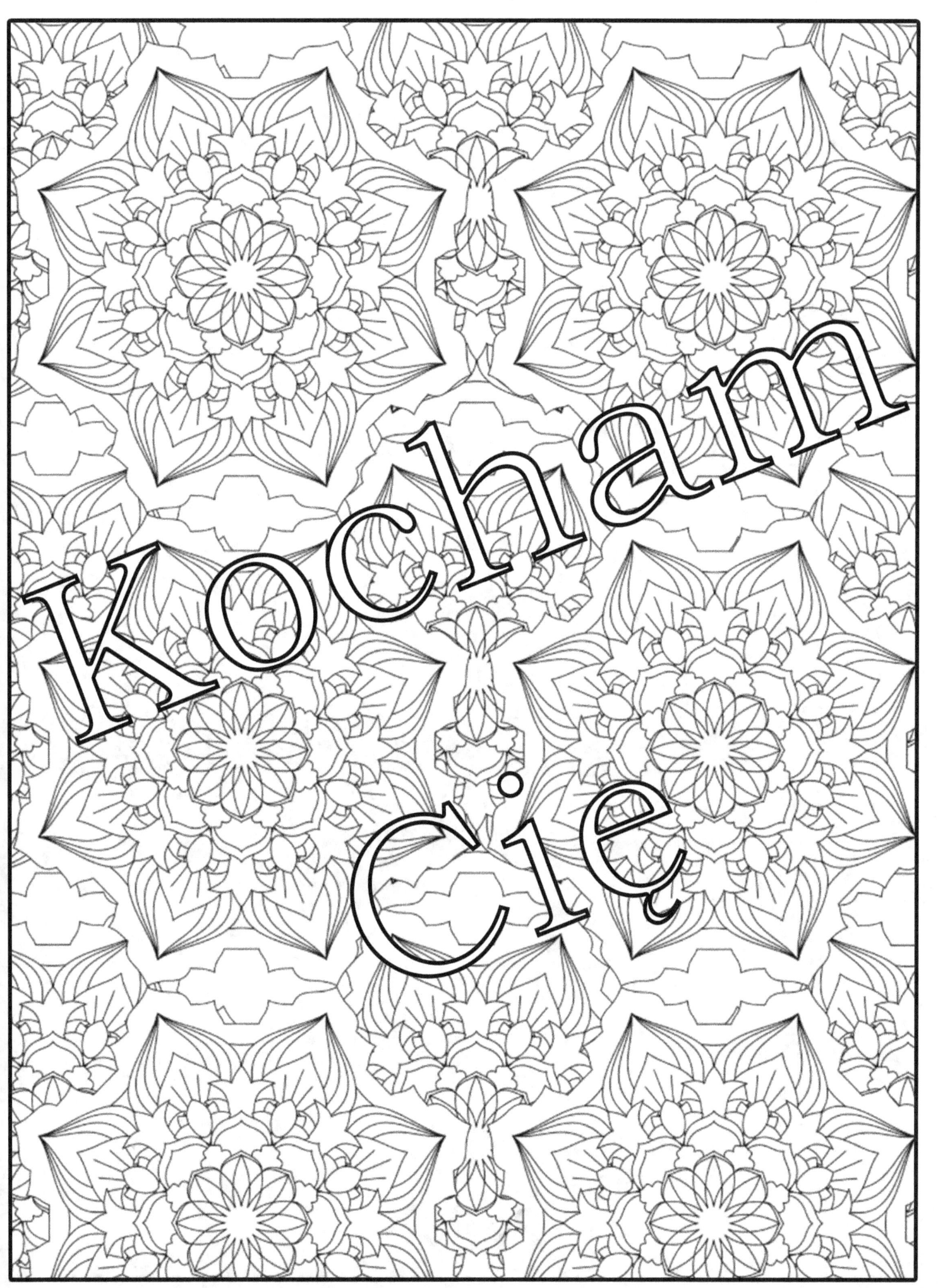

Polish

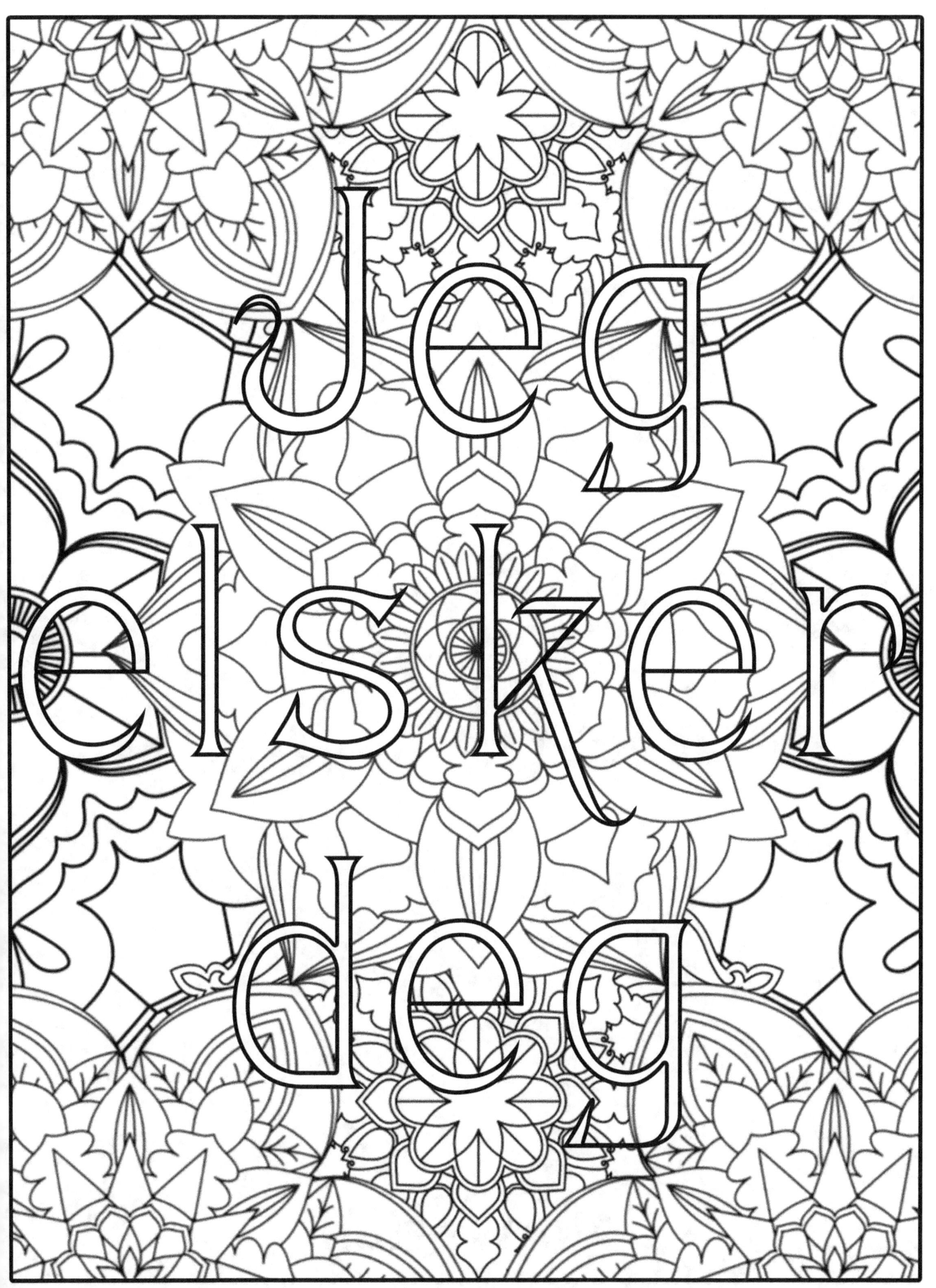

Norwegian

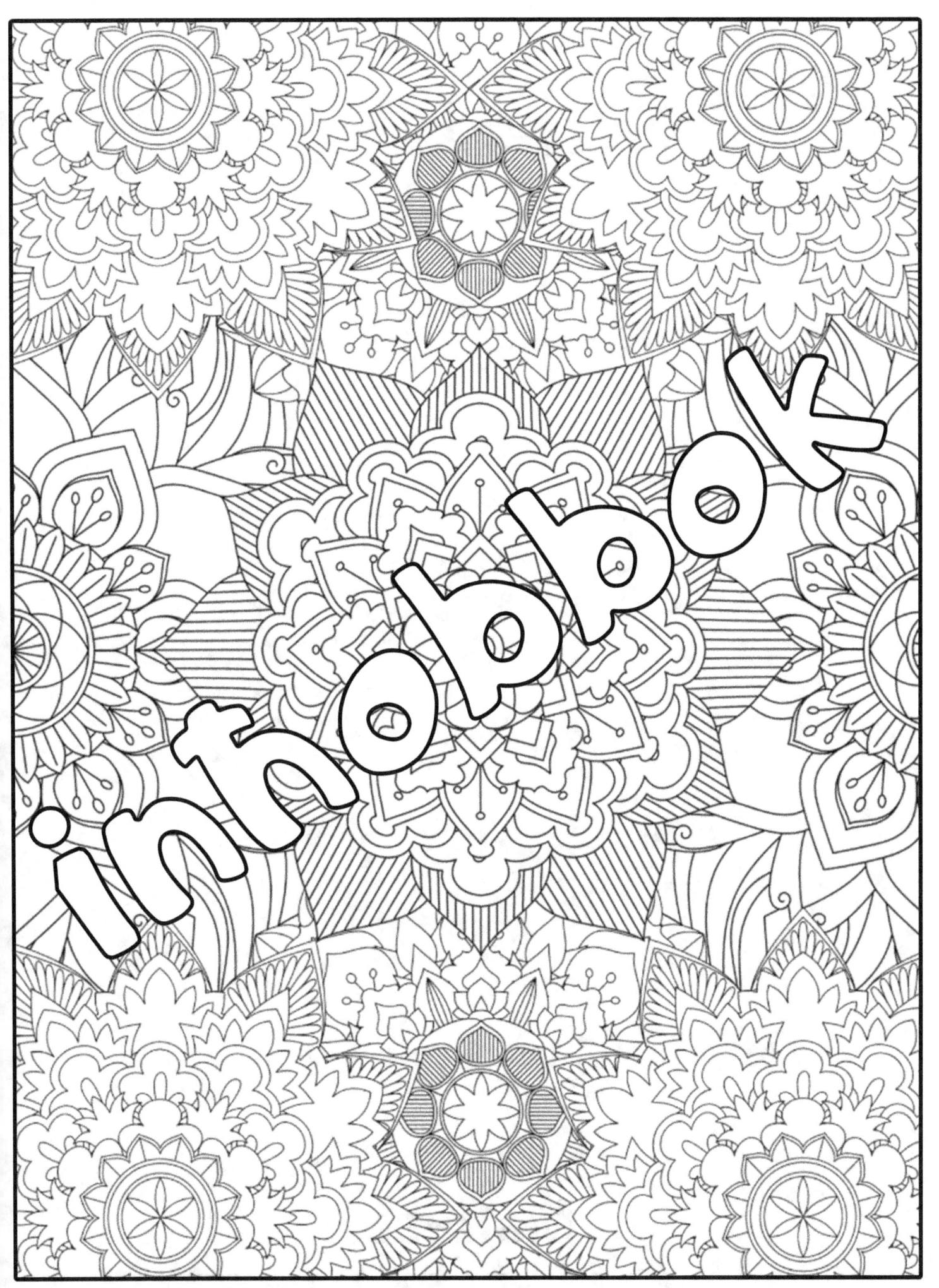

Maltese

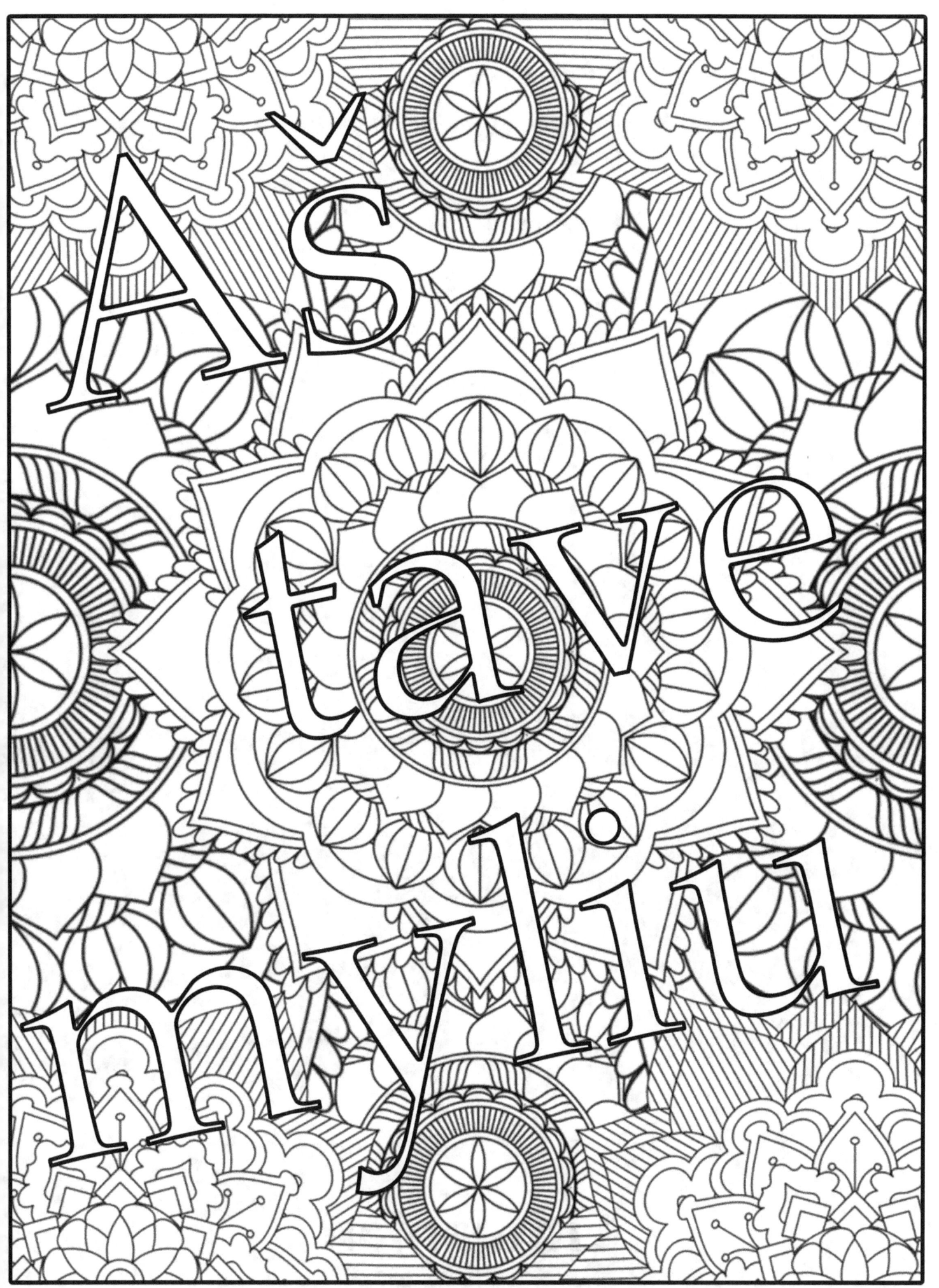

Lithuanian

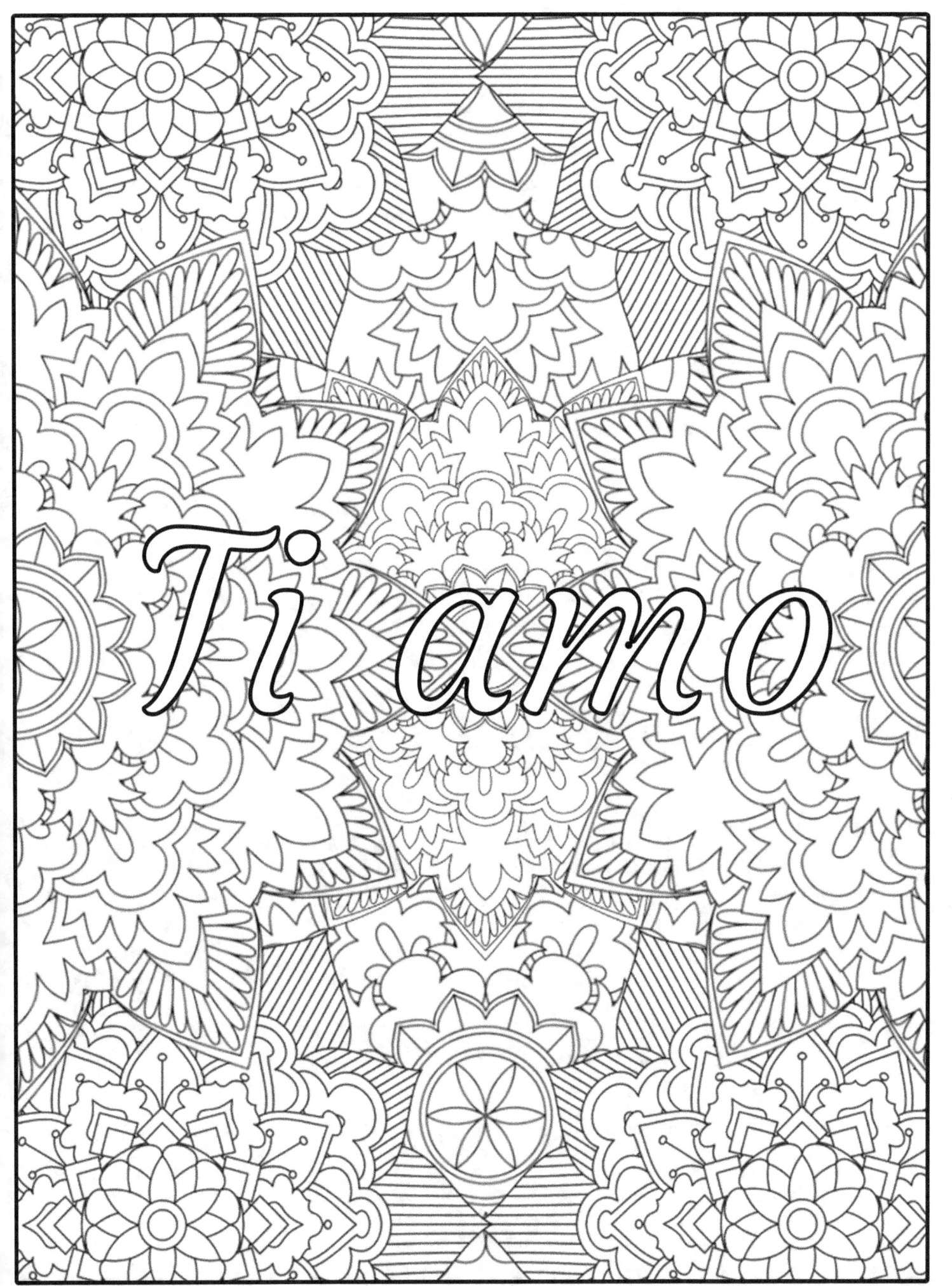

Italian

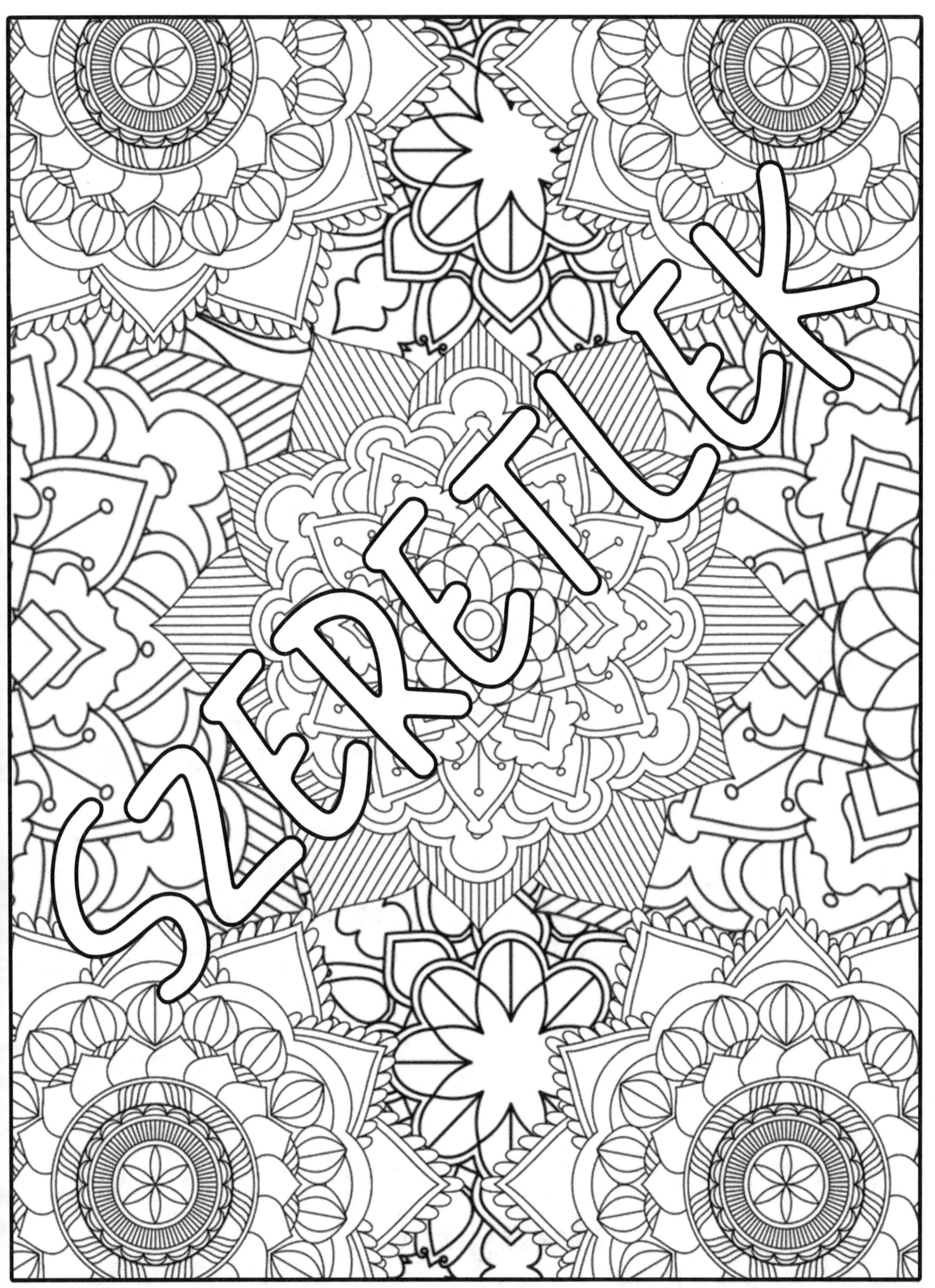

Hungarian

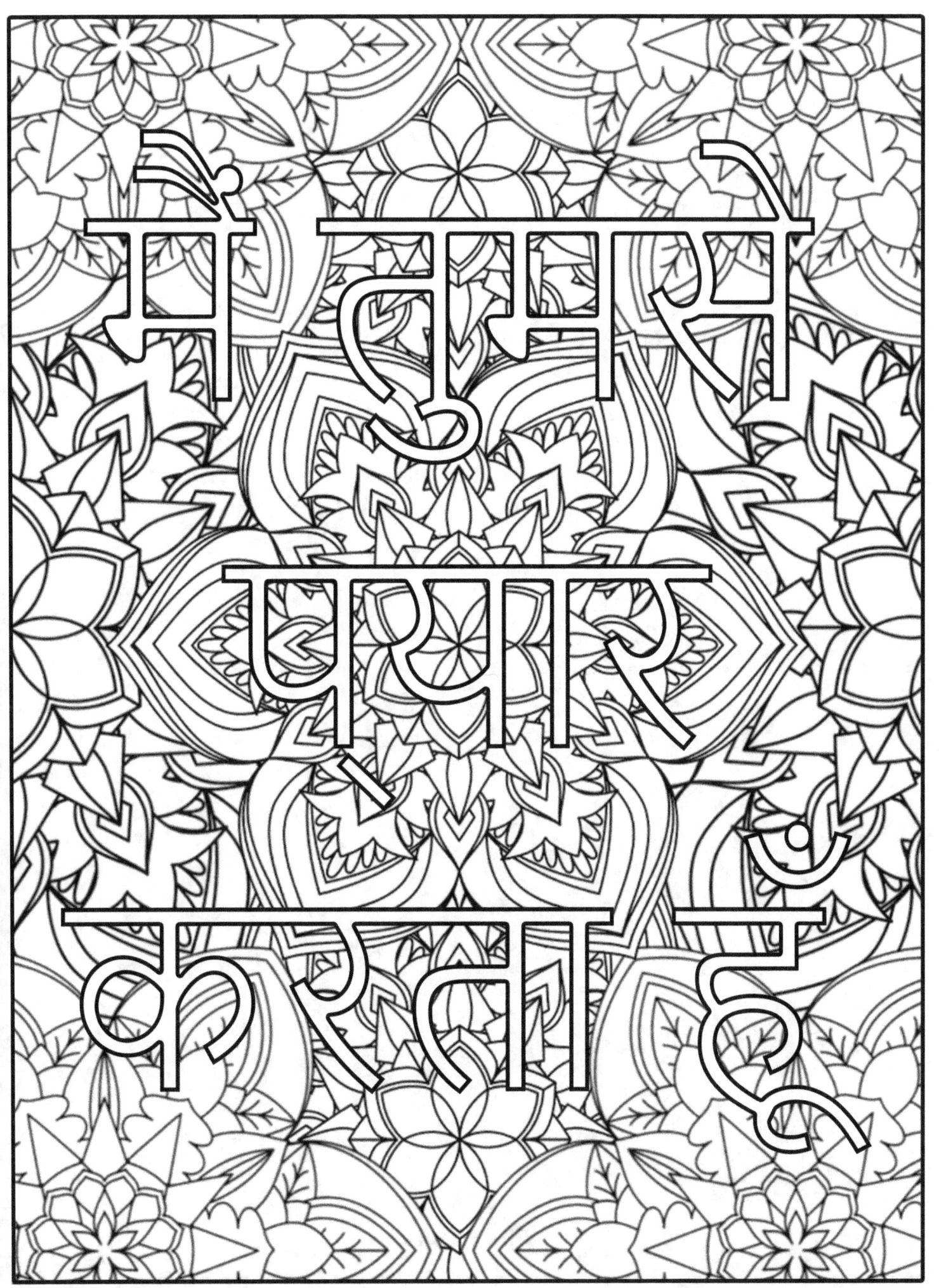

Hindi

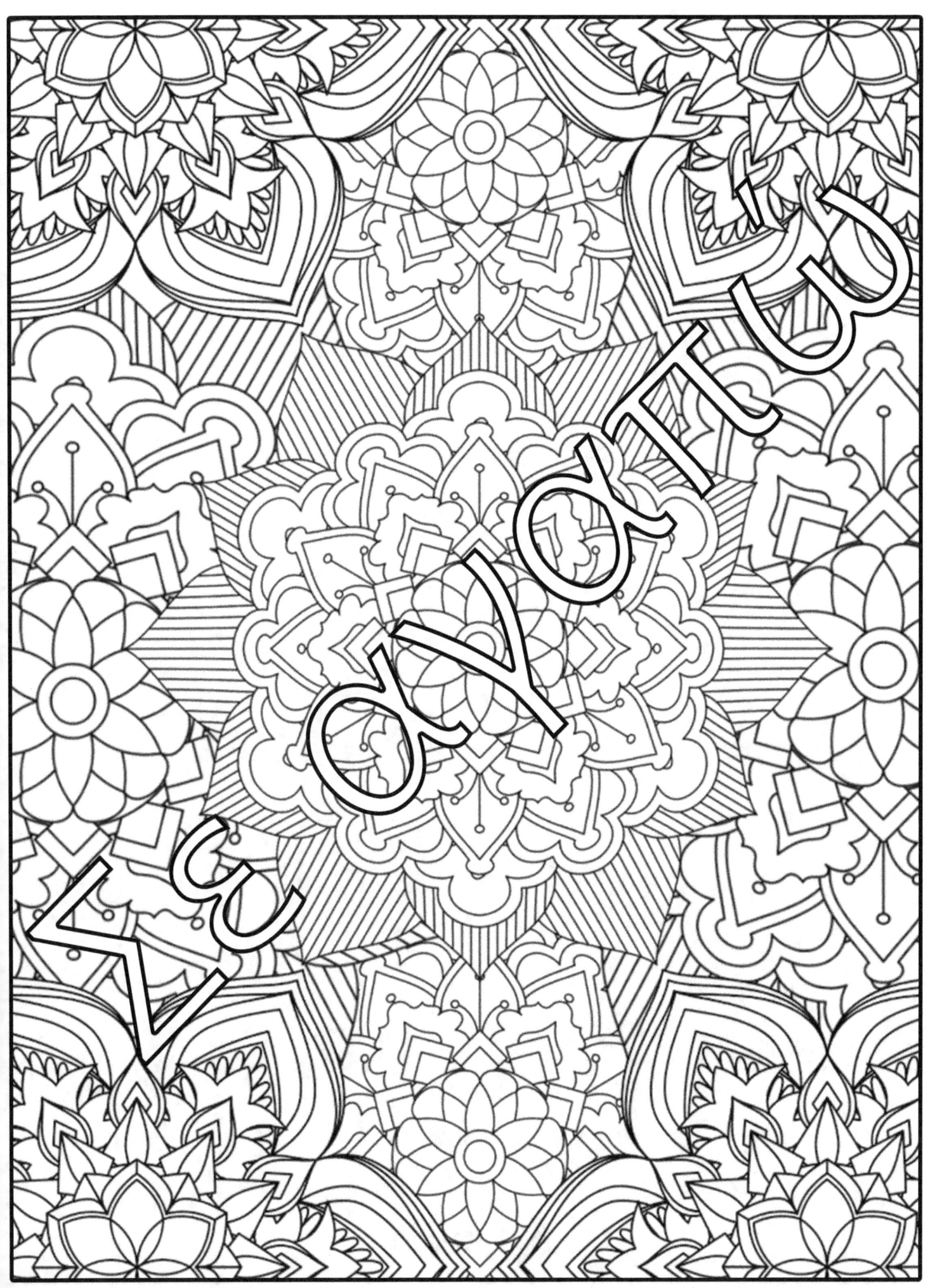

Greek

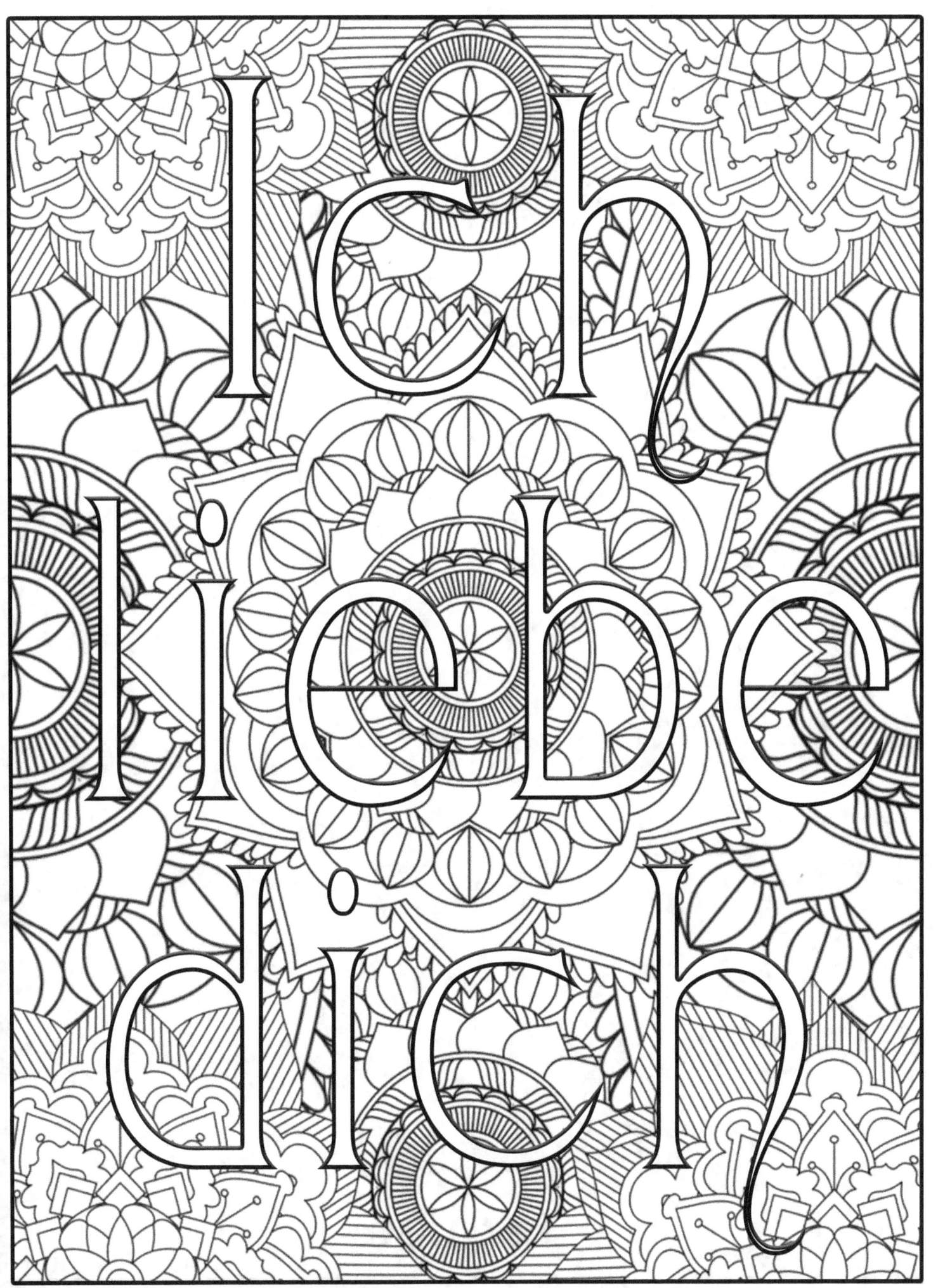

German

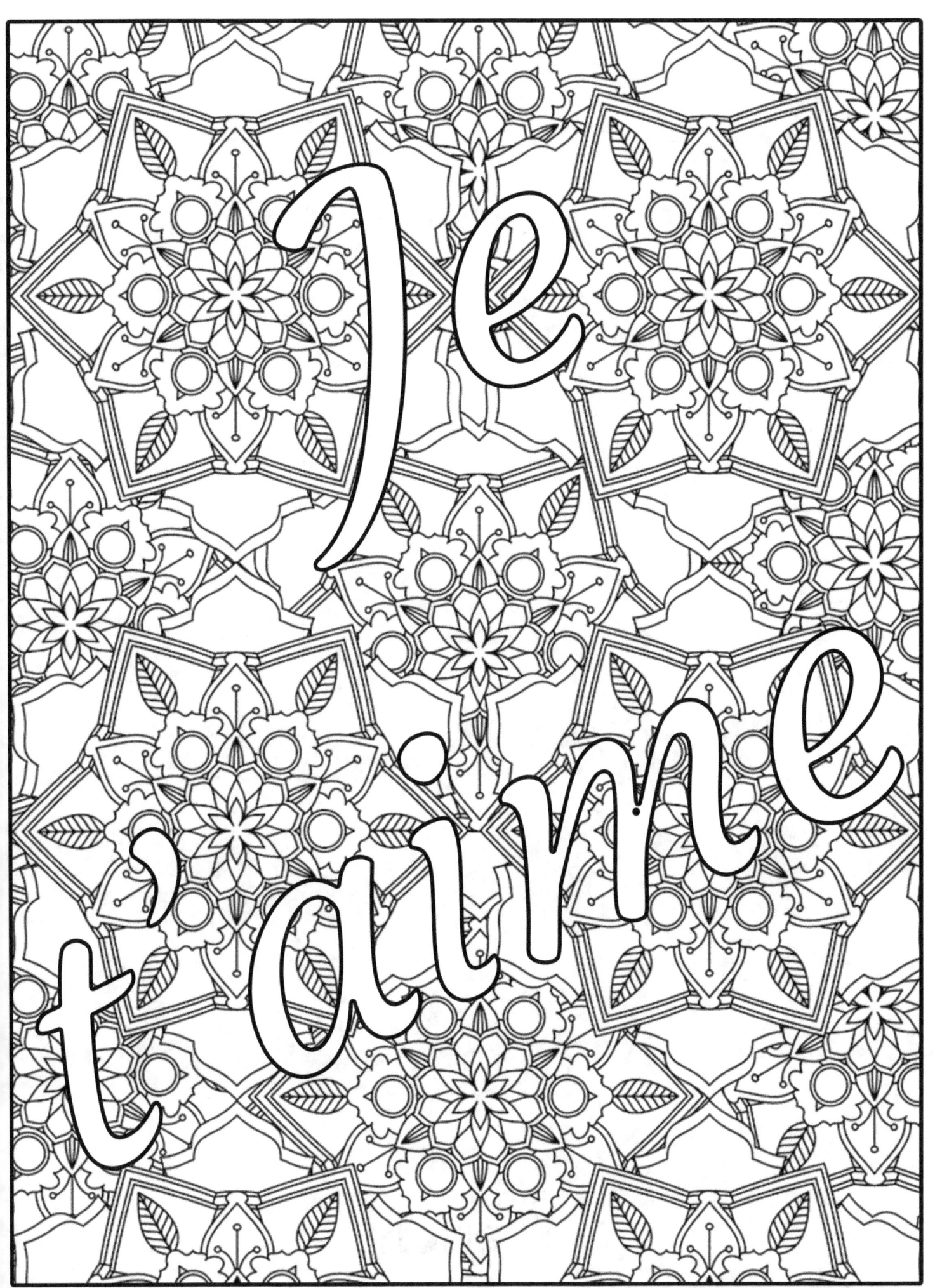

French

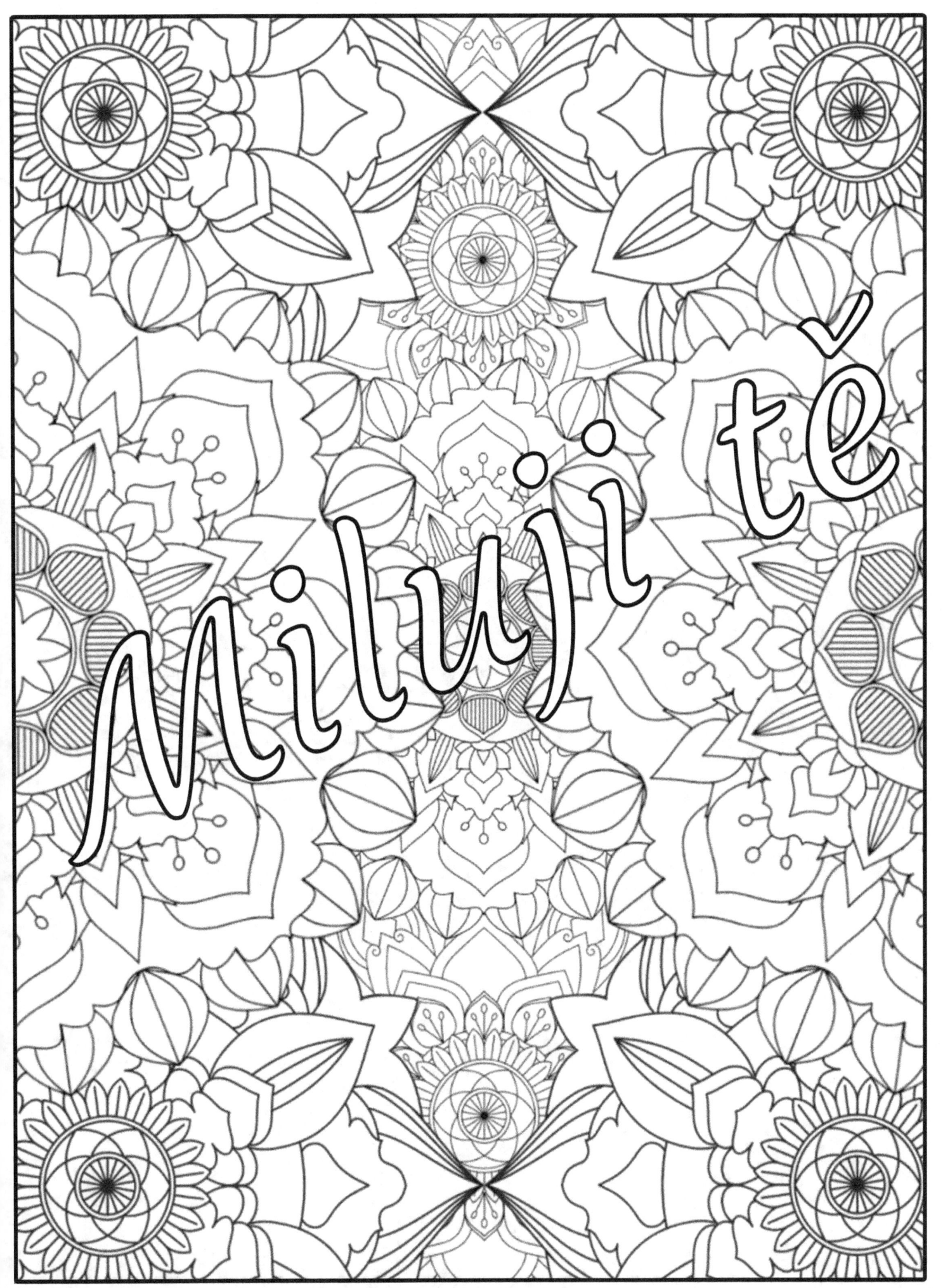

Czech

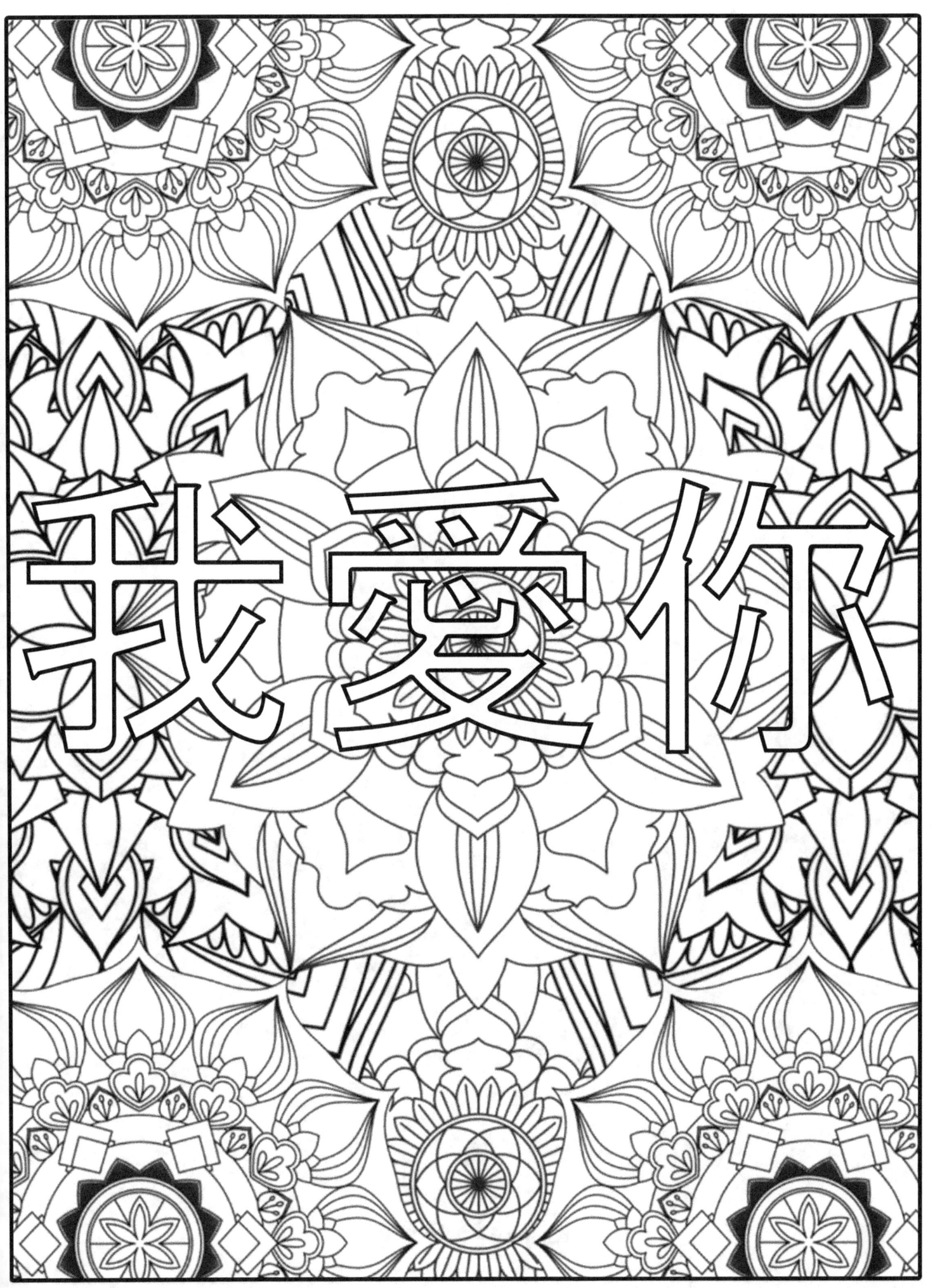

Chinese

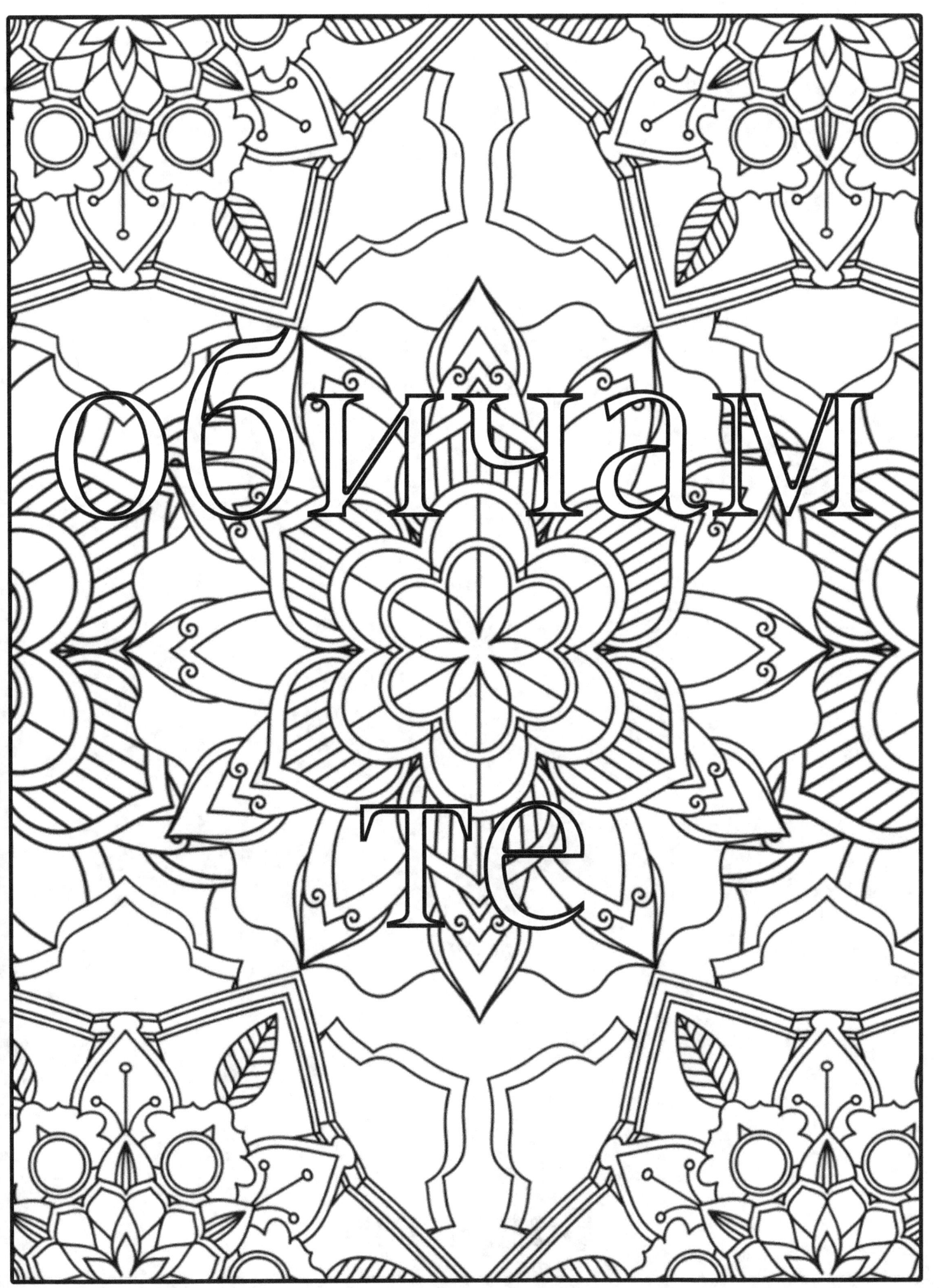

Bulgarian

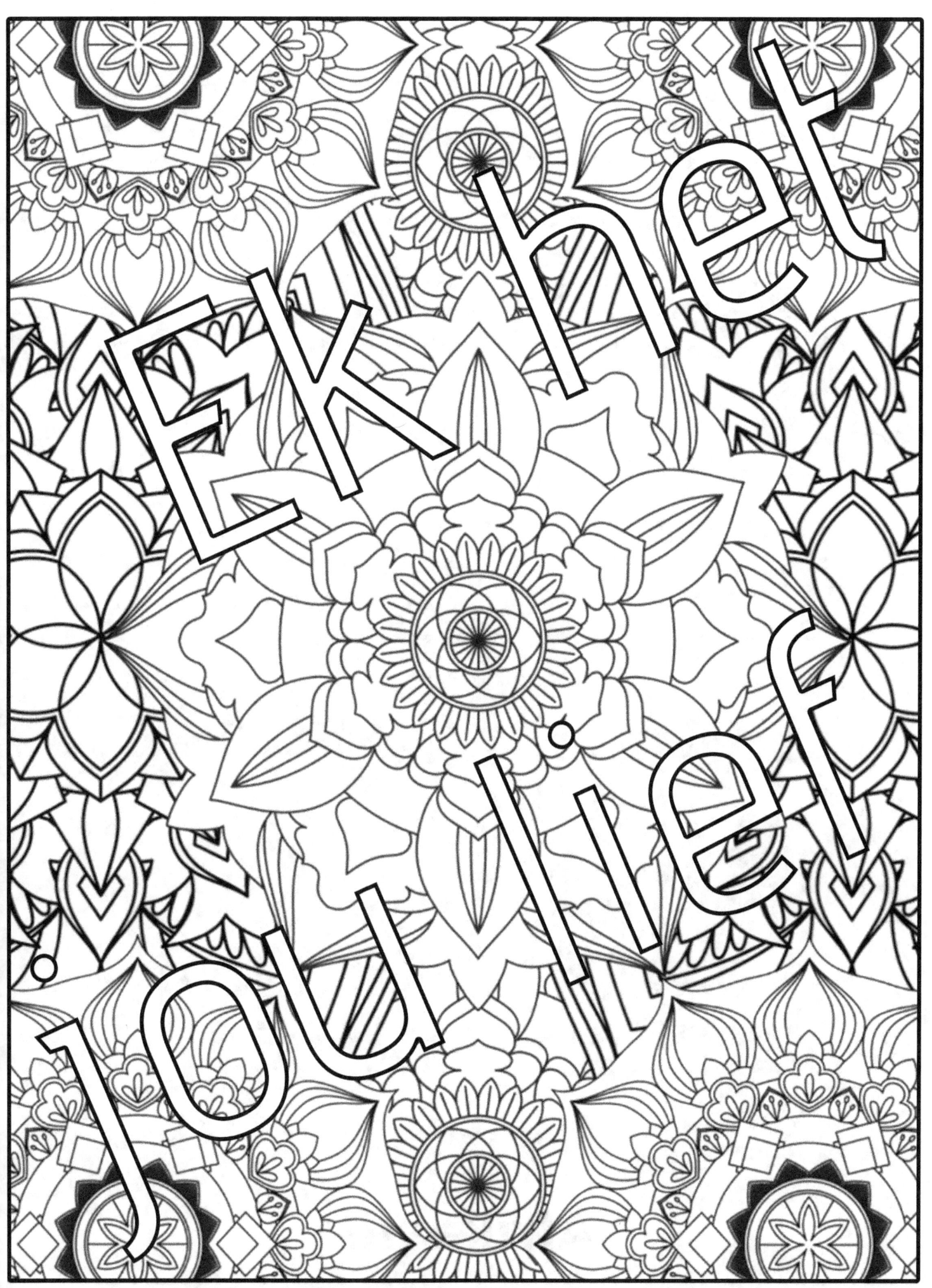

Afrikaans